How to Let Love Win!

How to Make Relationships Work!

Understandings, insights, tips and hacks!

Table of Contents

'If civilisation is to survive, we must cultivate the science of human relationships - the ability of all peoples, of all kinds, to live together, in the same world at peace.'

Franklin D. Roosevelt

1

Love Brings Up Anything Unlike Itself For Healing.

I nevitably when two people spend time together there will be disagreements, arguments and conflicts it's inevitable. The important thing is what you make it mean because the chances are they will continue because nobody can agree on everything all the time. What do you make them mean when they happen? Sometimes you get situations where people fall in love and the honeymoon period is happening and it's just great, and then something comes up, an issue comes and one or the other makes it mean something " look we're having a terrible argument we're not compatible it means that the relationship is not viable"!

Of course that isn't the case but that isn't the only way of looking at conflict. A great way of looking at conflict would be to give it the meaning that "love brings up anything unlike itself for the purpose of healing". It's because you've got a profound resonating feeling between you, that has given you a deep sense of safety, that deep rooted issues float to the surface for resolution and it by no means means that this relationship is not viable. In fact it means the opposite somehow there's something between you that creates a safety for these issues to come up and be resolved so that a deeper love, a deeper trust, a simpler way of being can evolve between you.

4

2

Psychological Entanglement Or Loving Relationship?

T here are two basic types of relationship. One we could call a psychological entanglement and the other is a loving relationship. There's a lot of psychological entanglements masquerading as loving relationships. Sometimes our relationships appear to have a mix of both.

A good way to describe the two types of relationship is how they are depicted in the ancient Tarot. In the Tarot they depict a loving relationship as two people who are not holding hands but are standing naked together with an angel above them in paradise. They are two sovereign individuals in their combined energy field being blessed by life. The other card is the devil card and that depicts two people again naked but chained together with the devil on top of them. That's the psychological entanglement, that's where projections happen, that's where transference happens that's where you have a thing called the Anima projection.

For a man, if your preference is women, you have an ideal feminine somehow in your unconscious mind maybe it's drawn from aspects of your mother maybe it's drawn from women that you have seen, maybe it's drawn from movies .

If I come across someone who embodies that ideal I will find that something literally pops out of me, a projection is projected out onto that person. They fulfil my ideal and so I get that they can receive my projection and I start to relate to them as my projection which is a subtle superimposition placed on them. This is done without realizing that you are doing it.

And it obviously happens the other way around so you can have one person projecting on one person or you can have both people projecting on each other and this feels like falling in love. Love at first sight.

When you launch a projection onto somebody it's like "the minute I saw her I knew".

I had this experience myself it caused me no end of bother until I distinguished it as a projection because it's quite different from actually being with someone in a conscious loving relationship where you are actually seeing the being as they are in full acceptance. When you are on the other side, when you're in the projection, you're not actually engaging with the person, you're engaging with your projection and they are always slightly mystified. They like the energy, they like the attention but they don't quite get it .They can't quite receive it.

The projection allows you to understand that part of you that had been suppressed and not really seen and you get to know it by projecting it out onto the other.

What is the course of a relationship that is fundamentally a projection? Generally it's very exciting to start with and it just really feels like this is it and it can be very passionate. Once the feminine is placed out it makes the male feel more male and the female is getting the the benefit of the projection because she is being idealised or even idolised and her more murky aspects are not being seen.

Fundamentally they're not actually engaging with each other but with projections. Then the passion can go negative there can be a lot of anger and resentment that comes up because the person obviously isn't who you've been projecting them to be, they've got their own personality and after a while they kind of get that they're not being got and it can cause really intense interchanges triggered by the smallest things.

When you launch your projection onto someone it really feels like this is it, this is the one and it isn't the one. Your' e actually experiencing a psychological dynamic. It is not the one and it is very hard to let go of that.

In the Tarot card you see they are chained together this means that you can't just walk away from it. Even if you walk away from it physically, because it was psychological in the first place, it still runs in you. This kind of pairing is very difficult to see and difficult to get out of.

A projection is often mistaken as love. Whereas love is something else in order to have a loving relationship we have to be free and complete in ourselves.

We have to have transmuted the neediness. How do we do that? How does a needy person let go of that neediness?

The answer is by returning to the Self, a moment in presence. You start to recognise that you don't actually need anything that you are already a complete being. This is the realisation that comes from being present to the Self.

You see that you are fulfilment, every time we come into the moment where we actually are the truth about us, that's fulfilment, it's complete, it's whole. There's nothing that we need there and spending time in this place starts to dissolve deep-rooted psychological neediness which comes out of a feeling that you haven't got everything that you need.

We become free as we move out of identifying as our psychological self, then our relationships become much simpler and much more authentic and profound.

3

Who Am I?

"The enquiry 'Who am I?' is the principal means to the removal of all misery and the attainment of the supreme bliss."

Ramana

If you're living as who you think you are,if you're living as an embodiment of the psychological self, somewhere in there there's the idea "I' m not good enough"," things don't work", or " there's something wrong with me". Then those deep rooted, primal negative thoughts will show up in everything. So you won't be good enough to have a loving relationship, you won't be good enough to have a happy life. It affects everything. So it's important that we really get the answer to this question "who am I?" very clear. Not just clear on the level of understanding but clear on the level of experience. Then we really can just put down a lot of baggage and what we can't put down presents itself, exposes itself naturally, in a beautiful process of Self- Realisation.

Self-Realisation is not about the psychological self, unraveling the knots of the psychological self. Self- Realisation is experiencing what's behind that, what's before that psychological self. This is the way that we turn from having psychological entanglements, to more and more having loving relationships. We could say that a loving relationship is when two people travel side by side through life together they're individuals and they're there's a vibration between them there's a beingness they share.

In a psychological entanglement masquerading as a relationship there can be multiple projections going on between the two people. For example if your relationship with your father or your relationship with your mother has not been resolved and accepted and released, then chances are you will attract someone that will allow you to project that unresolvedness. So you start actually responding to that person almost as if it's your mother or it's those qualities that you haven't resolved that are the basis of your relationship with your mother and likewise with your father.

Some people say that you can't expect to have a real loving relationship until you have completely resolved your relationship with your mother and your father because until then you will be subtly projecting it onto all primal relationships. In extreme cases, onto all relationships. So it's very clear, in order to have a loving relationship that's clear and simple and full of love and grows and flows, you have to first be clear about who are you, what is the Self and secondly to be able to release and let go and resolve any issues you might have coming from your childhood with your parents.

A psychological entanglement is not love. Love is different, a loving relationship is much more simple, it doesn't have this massive psychological content. You're not using the relationship to project out what you need to see of yourself onto the other or into the relationship. You're beyond that it's just two beings that are together flowing with space between them and this is an entirely different thing to the codependent psychological entanglement. To get over a psychological entanglement which is what most relationships actually turn out to be there has to be completion, you have to get what is going on, make conscious what was unconsciously driving you.

But don't worry, this again is something that happens naturally and beautifully once we make a commitment to truth, a commitment to knowing the Self and then our path through life appears as a journey toward love. It becomes easier to love as you realise that's really what you are and that the thing that was causing the complication was this false sense of self,this psychological self, this wounded self. If you're identifying as your wounded child, if you're identifying as being unloved, if you're identifying as being unlovable which would have come out of some experience you had in your childhood which you then gave the meaning to of not being lovable and not being wanted, then that will show up, you will attract people who don't want you. You will go for people who don't want you, who will abandon you. There are many different variations of this.

I had that very same thing in my earlier life. I had it that I wasn't wanted so I attracted someone who didn't want me and something was satisfied in attracting someone that didn't want me and the drama that ensued. It fulfilled a deeply held idea that I currently had about myself. Once it was exposed it never happened again.

What's amazing is that we can transform, there isn't a fixed way that we are. There is not any fixed way that we are!

We like to think there is! People say you've got patterns and you've got wounds from your past but who I am is not who the past says I am nor am I the psychological self.

In this moment, here now is the only place where life is real, is there a wounded child and can you call that child into this now? Do it, call it in, don't have it lurking in the shadows.

But that construct can't stand in the light, it can't make it into the full now, this moment, it can't come. You have to dive out of this moment into the past in order to re-experience it, it can't come into this now because it is only a memory,a construct. It will vanish.

This is the the principle of calling forth everything that you're running from and face it. Call it, call it forth whatever you're fearful of call it forward and watch it vanish.

4

Face The Fear

"He who is not everyday conquering some fear has not learned the secret of life." Ralph Waldo Emerson

I once had an experience when I was on Brighton Beach. The tide was very far out and there was a groin,like a jetty,a big concrete jetty coming out across the beach and when the tide was out I noticed that the very bottom of it there was a kind of archway door. I thought 'wow I've never seen that before I wonder where it leads'. So I went over to it and I went in. You go in and then suddenly you turn right and there's a tunnel going right the way through,

I wondered where it went, so I started walking towards the light.I noticed some movement and so then I started shouting "who's there?" and then no response came just a bit of echo and when I stopped, it stopped, so I walked on and it seemed to be getting bigger. It was getting a little bit scary now because I'm thinking maybe some drunk guy, maybe it's some guy carrying dark forces! I said "who's there? Who's there?" and I had this moment "do I turn back and leave it or do I just go on?" 'no' I thought 'I'll go on'. Then about two or three steps later I had the most astonishing realisation. What it was was my shadow,the light behind me was reflecting my shadow onto a wall in front of me where they blocked it off.

I was being scared by my own shadow but when I faced it I realised that it didn't actually have any reality what so ever and I had been projecting my fears onto that shadow.

That's really what it's like. So call it in, this moment is

always clear and full of light. Any shadow, call it, face it and you'll find that it vanishes.

Fundamentally you are freedom itself, you're whole, you're complete you lack nothing.

5

The Story Vs The Meaning

There's another distinction that's really important:

We have to distinguish between the story and the meaning.

So for example you have a big argument and the basis of the argument is 'you did this, youdid that, . You said this, you said that' and then the other person goes 'no you said, you said that ,you did this etc.' there's always two sides to the story.

When relationships break up or have a big argument you go and tell your friends what happened on one side and the other person tells their friends what happened on the other side and even though they shared the same experience each one is telling the story from a place of innocence blaming the other one for victimising them with their behaviour.

The thing to really understand is that there is no way that it was. You got it how you did he got it how he did and there is no objective truth about it.

Arguing about the story brings no good fruit.What needs to be communicated is what you made it mean, what are your needs and feelings.

The Truth is..

Who you're being that she is gives you how you get her,who you're being that I am right now is giving you how you're getting me. Who you're being that I am has given you how you're getting me. Everybody is getting me differently aren't they? There is no fixed way that I am.

Who you're being that you are gives you how you get yourself. You get yourself differently each time you encounter yourself. Why because who you're being that you are is changing.

What does it mean who you're being that something is? Who you're being that your partner is gives you how you get them, it means what kind of space you are for them determines how they appear to you. What you're allowing determines how they will turn up for you, what you're projecting on them will determine how you see them, how you're identifying them ,what you're thinking about them will determine how they turn up for you, if you've got negative thoughts about them that's going to affect how you perceive them which is going to be how you get them.

So this is important because the way we look at it ,we say "you are that way" and they go "no I'm not" "yes you are" "no I'm not".

The truth is that who I am being that you are is what gives me how I get you, there isn't a way that you are.

If there was it would be constant and we would all get you that way.

Your reaction to them is your responsibility, 'you make me feel this' no they don't! 'You make me think this' no they don't," you make me do this" no they don't!

This distinction can be really amazing if you start using it because then it's up to you, you take responsibility for how you're getting somebody and if you start looking into it you'll see that there are all kinds of payoffs as well and it opens up a whole new source for learning about your psychological self.

6

No One Can Betray You Without Your Permission.

Betrayal is one of the great victim stories in relationships: "he went off with someone else","she went off with my best friend"!

"He betrayed me" and everybody goes "oh my god that's terrible, that's awful isn't it". It is awful but no one can betray you without you giving them permission,without you inviting them to do that. Now obviously you don't invite them by going "oh yeah please betray me" in words!

It's more subtle, we don't just speak with our words that's one of the mediums we use to communicate to each other but we also use the way we're being.

Very often we have a complaint about our partner and we won't verbalise it because we don't want to rock the boat so it'll become something that comes in between the immediacy that we could be having and we kind of withdraw. That withdrawal could be counted as an invitation for betrayal. It might be a withdrawal of love or physical intimacies.

If someone feels that you have withdrawn from them and they don't know why,they will invent a reason why and also withdraw and then you'll pick up that they've withdrawn and then you will withdraw not really connecting it with the fact that you withdrew from them and then you'll withdraw further and so the next thing you know you've withdrawn from each other not really knowing why and love and intimacy have gone.

Withdrawal is a big statement, it turns love into being conditional, giving permission for betrayal.If you had a happy sex life and then something happened and the consequence was mutual withdrawal emotionally and physically, then the other person can take it that that is subtly giving permission for that person to go elsewhere to get their needs met. In a sense you're giving permission by who you're being in the relationship,no one can betray you without you having done that. You present yourself as a clearing for betrayal, you create yourself as a clearing for deceit and confusion, for things not working out. The unresolved unconscious mind is running the relationship.

The permission can come in many ways if you behave in such a way that the person thinks that they're not desirable or many times the betrayal is preceded by a change in the sexual dynamic.

In the beginning of a relationship perhaps there's a lot going on and then it may be after a while it settles down and then after a further while it gets sporadic and then maybe after a further while its stops altogether. Especially if there's not a lot of communication. There just isn't the intimacy on an authentic and real level for open-hearted giving,there's too much unexpressed, there's too much unprocessed and this gets in the way of the immediate intimacy.

So then someone might think "well you don't want me I'll find someone who does. You can't give me what I need so I'll go and get it elsewhere" and that is a response to how you were being, who you're being that your partner is gives you how you get them.

If you get them as betraying you that's coming out of who you're being,the clearing you were for them, the space you were for them.

Now this is a stand you can take, this is a perspective you can occupy and it's a very powerful one because it gives you power. If you take the position "oh my partner betrayed me I'm a victim of his behaviour and now I'm terribly upset" then there's not really a lot you can do with that. Obviously in the beginning when we have a deep emotional shock by all means take refuge in the victim "oh he did this" and gather people around, this is what we always do, we gather our friends around and we tell them the story from our point of view about how we were victimised by the behaviour of the partner who betrayed us.

It's important that as soon as you feel strong enough you take responsibility because this is how you'll get closure, this is how you'll be able to move on from that incident.

Who were you being that you were such that he felt it was okay to do that to you?

How dare he? He did it but you gave him permission by who you were being that youwere "I'm the sort of person that gets betrayed." That beingness attracts people who betray you.

Who were you being that the relationship was such that betrayal featured in it?

Sometimes these things are really potent. Like with jealousy for example, when you're being jealous of somebody "you looked at that girl, you know you shouldn't have looked at that girl" quite often the person themselves isn't thinking about betraying the love emotionally, energetically or physically, they're not thinking about it but the jealousy comes in. Who you're being that they are is that they're the sort that would do that, so then they start to turn up for you like that but originally they had no intention of being like that. So it's a very potent thing, who you're being that somebody is gives you how you get them, it's kind of counterintuitive but it is actually how it plays out.

Now that's not to say that the person who did the betraying, who went off with someone else is innocent. They've got to look at who they're being that their partner was, they've got a story there too or something to understand and the two can be completely different.

When in a relationship with another person you will be experiencing the same drama but getting a completely different meaning from life, completely different teaching from life. We can never really know what the teaching for the other person is and that's another thing in relationships. I remember some guru saying "If you're clearer about your partner's psychological state than your own, you're in big trouble"!

Often we spend our whole time trying to figure out where the partner is at and what their psychological position is when really the only thing we can really look at, that's going to really have a big impact, is us and who we're being that the relationship is and why.

It's a horrible thing betrayal it really undermines your sense of yourself if who you're being that you are is coming out of your psychological self.

So when people betray you it's because you gave them invitation to by who you were being. We have blind spots, we're not always conscious of how we're being or more accurately who we're being that something is which gives us how we get it. We're not conscious of it,we just see it reflected in the result. So that's where to look why did he betray me? Don't look to him look to you.

The main thing is that there isn't actually a fixed way that anything is, but it appears that there is and it appears that it is because we are the ones generating that appearance.

I remember back in the day there was this girl and who I was being that she was was such that I never got her. But I really wanted her and she actually came into my social circle and had sex with lots of my friends but I really loved her and I didn't get her. Before that I pretty much got everybody that I wanted and it was a big shock. Now looking back I clearly see who I was being that she was gave her a total invitation to be that way with those people and me. I invited her to be that way by the way I was being because the truth was that I was dancing with my projection and not her. What I needed from her psychologically wasn't sex and all the rest of it, it was to project this complex for healing. I had a script of being unwanted from my childhood that I was living out, that was surfacing in this drama.

That's what happens if we don't realise where we're at within.Then the teaching comes with greater and greater density. First the truth comes as a flash, an insight and if you're honest and get the flash you can get the whole thing very quickly on the subtlest of levels and move on, but generally we don't and so it comes slower,more dense thoughts and dreams and then if we still don't get it then life gives us a drama in which it plays out. That's what was happening with me,I was playing out this idea of being unwanted and unlovable.

So she wouldn't necessarily have been like that, she was available, she was doing whatever she was doing but who I was being that she was gave me this unique experience of her that wasn't really who she was to herself or how others got her.

I learned from that,who you're being that relationships are gives you how you get them. If who you're being that who you are is that you're not good enough then you're likely to attract a relationship that proves that right.

Somewhere in the story of the relationship would be you showing up as not good enough. Is that the truth about you? Well you might think it is and you might say well "no

I actually am not good enough because look at my past, that happened and it proves I wasn't good enough and in fact I've got a whole trail of not being good enough throughout my life."But that's who the past says you are and all of those things came out of the beingness of not being good enough not out of the reality that you're not good enough. A lot of people never get to that point where they make that distinction.

Just because you show up as not good enough doesn't mean that you're actually not good enough, just because your relationships continuously fail doesn't mean that you can't be great at relationships. Who you're being that relationships are gives you how you get them. There isn't a way that they are but who you're being that they are gives you how they appear for you.

Once you recognise that it was who you were being - a space where that kind of result was inevitable.You can see what the payoffs for doing it were and then transform it.

7

The Listening Agreement

"Listening is an art that requires attention overtalent, spirit over ego, others over self."

Dean Jackson

We have this desire, to keep it all peaceful; "I am feeling things but I don't think I'm going to communicate them because it will destabilize the relationship" but if you don't communicate it compounds and gets more and more of an obstruction,the next thing you know is that you've really grown apart from that person. It'snot that you don't love them or it's not that their original connection isn't there,it's just that there's so much stuff that hasn't been shared. It's really important to communicate because if you don't the relationship will lose its depth and its longevity to the degree that you don't communicate. If you don't communicate resentment builds up and then comes bursting out angrily achieving very little and very often making things worse.

Not much comes out of arguing but there is a need for real communication and the best way that I have found for that and I've suggested this to many people and they've done it and reported back to me that for them also it really works.They tell me it is the foundation of a new culture of communication in their relationships.

There's a thing called the Listening Agreement.When you feel an argument coming on,you feel a tension coming, you identify it and recognise it and then choose to have it not go down the road into an argument but instead to invoke the Listening Agreement.

This is what Love looks like when its winning! The Listening Agreement is a wonderful thing it's where you say to your partner "look I' m not feeling good, could we invoke the Listening Agreement" and he agrees and so that means you sit opposite each other so that you can have eye to eye contact and feel each other across a table. (It's not good to do it when you're drunk!). Then the person agrees that they will listen to you,remaining in contact with you and listening without interruption until you have fully expressed what it is that you need to express. Then the deal is that when you are finished and it can be as long as you need with silences, then he will have his say and he will speak back to you with just your full attention and no interruption.

This is so incredible because one of the things that happens when we come out of alignment in a relationship is we stop looking at each other. The amount of time since you last looked at your partner properly and saw them can go into days and weeks even if you're living with the person. You're always not really getting them, looking at them or connecting to them. Communication becomes superficial.

With the Listening Agreement the first thing that happens is you look into your partner's eyes. You put your sword and your shield down for a moment, the sword of attacking and the shield of defending,you can put that down and just give your full attention to your partner and your partner will blossom in your attention.

It's a very powerful thing the gift of your listening.

Usually what happens when you do that is you start to look into the

24

person's eyes and they're giving you their attention and somehow you get reconnected,you get realigned to what the real dynamic between you is.

When you're not arguing but listening and looking you tend not to come from an of egoic, competitive place because the root of arguing very often is needing to be right in order to preserve your ego's stance. But when you sit opposite each other and one of the partners is giving full listening,the communication tends to come from your heart and the listening encourages that and becoming present to the other person.

Present to what you're feeling and present to your deeper values. So the quality of what is communicated has a much better chance of being real and authentic and useful.

After you've said whats in your heart you give your full listening to your partner without interruption. It's just wonderful when people feel heard. Sometimes that is literally all you needed to do.

"Deep listening is the kind of listening that can help relieve the suffering of another person. You can call it compassionate listening. You listen with only one purpose: to help him or her to empty his heart."

Tich Nhat Hanh

In those kind of conversations your story about what's happening is not the greatest thing you could communicate! "Well you did this and then you did that" it's not the greatest thing to communicate because it's always going to be you as the hard done by one or it's always going to be from your perspective. They don't want to hear about your analysis of them,they don't really want to hear your analysis of the relationship,they just want to know where you're at now and what you got from all that about yourself. There isn't a way that the drama was it's how you got it but what's important to communicate,what really works in that Listening

Agreement situation is when you talk about what you need and what you are feeling.

Your partner isn't obliged to give what you need to you but at least they know and very often when people are told what their partners need they are inclined to give it. Often it had not occurred to the other what your needs actually are and they'll try that just because they want to love you. Then the kindness thing starts to happen again and that is so great.

In my last relationship my partner was so kind, she did kind things and I found it really confronting because it showed up how how mean I was in a very subtle way, not like grand meanness but with subtle meanness in terms of not being very generous with with my doings in the relationship. So this was something tremendously valuable,her kindness inspired me to be like that.It awakened kindness in me, that's one of the things that gave the relationship great value to me because I realised kindness as a currency in a relationship in a way that I hadn't before.Everyone can be kind if they choose to be especially if they know what you need.

The Listening Agreement is one of the most powerful tools for Letting Love Win! Please try it at least once!

With the Listening Agreement you both take the time to really listen to the other without interruption for as long as they need and then they listen without interruption to you.

Whilst you are doing that a subtle realignment takes place, you may notice your body language starts to synchronise and dance, then your breathing harmonises with the other and before you know it your hearts have quietly opened to each other again and there are tears of joy as with held emotion releases and the love is restored!

8

Are You Lovable?

A re you a place where love can happen, a clearing for love? Could someone love you just exactly as you are right now or do you have to change first before are you lovable?

When you ask yourself that question it's 'yes'isn't it and if something comes up well then look at that because that's interesting "oh I'm too fat,oh I'm too old, I am, but why would anybody want me? I'm not as beautiful as I was, I haven't got any money, I am too set in my ways."

All these reasons come up and get in the way of being loved. The truth is though however you see yourself there are people who are in great relationships who are fatter than you, crazier than you, poorer than you!

If you're continuously having relationships that fail and choosing wrong ones then you need to look at yourself, you need to look at "what is my root thinking about me in relationships?" Who you're being that relationships are is giving you how you're getting them.

God isn't saying "oh no that person, not gonna give her love, I'm not gonna give her a long loving relationship, she did that, no I'm not, I'm gonna punish her'. God is not like that, the universe isn't like that, you are the generator of these experiences in relationships and if you trace it back you can see who you're being and where it came from.

It wasn't always this way.

Typically what happens is we get in a relationship maybe the first one way back then or whenever, and it goes pear-shaped and then in that traumatic moment of being heartbroken we do a lot of thinking about ourselves we do a lot of thinking about us and relationships. But because we're heartbroken we come up with all kinds of nonsense but it seems real "oh I don't know what it is but there's just something wrong with me,I think I'm wounded,I think it was my parents fault,I think it was my childhood,I just don't seem to be able to work with relationships,I always choose wronguns and so they always break down,"

Those thoughts, that have arisen out of trauma and misery,get taken as accurate assessments of reality of who you are and they are not. But we don't realise that so it just compounds the ideas that relationships don't work,that Im not good enough. Then another one turns up who's picked up on that vibe that you're a clearing for and comes in and proves it again, does the same thing again.Perhaps in a different way and the end result again is proving your deepest negative thought about yourself right.

You need to get a new thought about yourself because it's not who you are, there isn't a way that you are. Who you're being that you are will give you how you get yourself and it's as simple as that. Seeing that you've got everything you need to have a beautiful loving relationship.

Once you get out of the mindset,once you expose the mindset that's obstructing you having happy relationships, compassionately seeing that it's built of nonsense which arose, sounding like common sense, in a time of emotional trauma. You're not broken there's nothing wrong with you.

Recognising your self as Presence you can then take an objective look at the psychological self and see who you have been and that it all stemmed from thoughts and meanings you created about yourself in a time of trauma.

These thoughts were informed by the trauma,mostly in the early part of your life and not by the reality of who you truly are.

Presence is when you are not in your mind but awake in this now as an emanating being.

What attracts love is a being who is open to it, who's not besieged by negativity in the matter of relationships and who recognizes that they're lovable just as they are.

What does that mean being lovable? Being a place where love can happen.

The training for that is daily kindness. The training is important because as you get older if you don't watch out you become more unlovable. You're just not a place where it can happen, you get cantankerous, cynical and jaded. The antidote to that is daily kindness and returning to Presence again and again.

Concentrate on maintaining your kindness, lovability and your caring. Steppingout of frozenness, stepping out of your comfort zone, reaching into others lives every day as a way of being. You make sure that you're keeping your love light alight by caring about people, by being kind to people, by empowering people, by encouraging people, by acknowledging people. Basically giving what you want to get that's the way that you create yourself as a being that is lovable.

It's amazing the difference you can make with a beautiful comment, with a kind comment you can change someone's whole day. So if you're not in a relationship right now or if you are, then that's the training. Share the love and be kind.

9

Are You Loving?

Are you a loving being? Most people think they are and most people are because we are, that's our nature. The thing to get clear is that being lovable and being loving is that it's now, just as you are. It's not when I've dropped a stone in weight I'll be totally lovable or when I've got a new dress or when I've got more money.

Right now because love doesn't need a reason, it's magic, it's a gift, it's a grace from life.

Just when you think it's not going to happen it happens. That's what happened to me, I thought 'I've had a really good innings with relationships,' I thought 'well probably now I'm kind of done', and then out of the blue the best relationship I ever had came, for four years and it was a beautiful relationship and I would say it was one where more than ever before, it was not a psychological entanglement, it was loving awareness. Two beings flowing and not getting entangled.

So you never know when it's gonna happen. Astrology doesn't tell you, sometimes it does and it still doesn't happen. Love is a mysterious and wonderful thing and you are lovable that's the point to get. You're lovable just as you are. Even though you are still in process, still haven't sorted out your your brokenness, still got strange habits, still got strange protocols, still got complexes and fears and all kinds of stuff but you are still lovable.

Still lovable and you can be loving and it makes us realise that being loving and being lovable,they're separate,they're deeper than our psychology,its on a soul level. It doesn't really matter who you are.If you look around you see people that are clearly psychologically unstable but they're in love relationships. You can see people who have got unattractive bodies by standard definition and they're in great relationships .So it's more about who you're being,are you a place where Love could land?

Do you know who are you being that you are in the matter of relationships? Are you being that it's a real possibility for you just as you are? If you're not then you can invent that possibility, you can get that it's actually is possible. "I am lovable and I am loving".

Please remember that nobody's touch is like your touch,nobody's smile is like your smile, nobody's laugh is like your laugh, nobody cares like you care, your mother doesn't care like you care, your sister doesn't care like you, only you care that way. These are some of the wonderful, unique things about you.

If you think too much about yourself you will only see yourself as what can be thought about and you'll forget the things that can't be thought about like what it's like to be in your presence, like your brand of kindness. These are tremendously important parts of you,heart qualities. You have a heart, you have a loving heart that is not broken that is not damaged that cannot be damaged.

Looking out for others, being kind. Who are you when you're kind? When you're being kind you're so lovable!

It's one of the really attractive things about you,your kindness did you know that? How beautiful you are when you're being kind.How beautiful you are when you're listening,when you care what someone's got to say, you care about them, you've got time for them.Your are a space and have a listening for them. You are so lovable when you're like that authentically.

Trying to be a certain way? Not so lovable. Acting like you think lovable looks like? No, not so great! Coming from your psychological wound? Not very lovable.Being needy? Not very lovable.

Find your freedom,find the Self, the whole Self that you are. You're not wounded, your wound is only psychological,your wounded child is a psychological construct,a designation given to a group of thoughts, memories and behaviours, it's not actually wounded,you've grown up now!

People can't complete you, it's not when you get the great relationship that you will be complete this is the source of neediness.

You can only do that for your self.Circumstances won't do that. You have to be complete if you want to have a loving relationship.You have to be a place where that can happen which is clear and disentangled from the past.

We can resolve the past and stillness is where the past gets resolved.

You don't have to work your way through every issue of your psychological self in orderto become free of it. You just have to realise what it is and that you're the observer of it once you see it objectively then your interest in it is not quite as great as it was because you're no longer identifying as it.You're just seeing it as as something other than your Self as now you recognise your Presence as the true Self.

You still are as you always were Freedom itself, Awareness. Get back there, that is the Awakening and with that happy relations,with that ,miracles and wonders.

Being really and truly what you are then you will attract someone else who's on that same kind of level and you will flow in this much more simple way, feeling much more love. When you flow as a complete being with another complete being and you haven't collapsed into each other, you haven't created co-dependencies, when you realise there's no one actually there, you can really relax and just be with the other being. You are complete, your fulfilment comes from within you every time you're present. There's nothing really to work out.

You become disenchanted with trying to figure out the psychological self.It's unfigurable, it's unfixable! There are some things that you can look at and get some clarity on and are helpful but basically the way out of suffering, the way out of the misery, the way out of attachment, the way out of the obsession is to recognise what the Self truly is-Presence.

This idea that you have of yourself is not who you actually are. The idea you've built up, this construct, is not actually who you are and as long as you identify as that there will be suffering and dysfunctional relationships.

When you open up to that Awakening and recognise Presence and choose to live as Presence, to get comfortable with emptiness, then life becomes wonderful.

Once you get that kind of possibility for yourself, you've created a clearing, you've created a space for Love and it'll start to open up and the next thing you'll get synchronistic signs that you're lovable and that it can happen. Then it does.

10

The End Game Card

I nevitably in relationships people will have contre temps, they will have arguments, there will be times when harsh words are spoken.

Points want to be made and the feeling that the other one isn't really getting what you're saying can be really annoying. That's when we have the tendency to get dramatic and play the Endgame card.

In the whole pack of the ways and things that can happen in a relationship one of those cards is the Endgame card. We use it when we are furious slam it down and go well that's it "f.ck right off its over I am leaving!"

This card should be taken out of the pack and put in a drawer and you only go to that drawer when you're calm. There may come a point where your relationship does end, the time has come for it to end for whatever reason but that should never happen in the heat of anger. Never use the Endgame Card as a way of making your point or hurting your partner.

Keep the Endgame Card, the end of the game card, keep that somewhere else and never use that when you're having a heated argument only use it when things calm then you say 'okay maybe it's time for us to part'.

Then it will be real, then it will have power. So many times people use that card then, after a few minutes even they don't feel that way anymore but because of pride they can't come back.

11

Anger Management

"If you were easier on yourself, you wouldn't be so tough on everyone else."

Kate McGahan

I t's very important to realise that when these differences come between people there's a principle which is that 'people are never angry about what they're angry about'.

This means that what they are saying they are angry about actually is just a trigger for a deeper pre-existing anger that they have not dealt with.

Anger and rage serve a function and that function is to point us to an issue that needs to be recovered, perhaps a memory that is hidden deep in the unconscious but needs to be found and resolved. Then the anger disappears.

There are no angry babies. If you can remember that you wouldn't then have to react about it or have to take it so personally. It's only when you take their anger personally that you get sucked in.

People are always talking about themselves even when they're shouting at you!

12

Don't Characterise

There was a woman who called the other day and she wondered why she kept getting dumped after the third date and after a lot of unwinding what really became clear was that she was characterising the relationship and insisting on the other doing the same too early. After the third date she thought they should be talking about futures, defining what stage they were at in terms of getting committed, then engaged, asking how much the other loved etc.

Don't characterise the relationship,let it grow naturally without being defined and quantified by an anxious mind.

In fact don't characterise yourself, just be who you are, don't characterise your partner, don't tell your partner who he is, don't tell your partner who she is, it's really annoying and actually rude unless you have been invited to make those kinds of judgements and comments. They know who they are, they live with themselves all the time,they don't need you to make characterisations of them,have some courage and flow with them in the feeling of being you both create..

Don't fight over how you characterise the relationship, there is not a fixed way that the relationship actually is, so it's not a question like your version,your characterisation is the right one and his characterisation is the wrong one or vice versa. There isn't a truth about it, it just is what it is for each of you, you will always get it differently and thats fine.The characterisation is always an approximation and never the reality.

Leave everything free and spacious,let there be lots of space in the relationship, don't define it because when you define it then you're going to have arguments because almost certainly the way you see it's not going to be the way you partner sees it, so don't characterise it- live it, feel it and don't let your mind get hold of it.It really does not mean anything if he sees it differently to you.

Maybe it doesn't sound like it's very important whether you're characterising or you don't characterise but it is because it drags a free flowing feeling into the mind and asking someone to characterise how they are felling about everything when they maybe do not even know themselves yet can have a negative effect, Its better to let nature and chemistry work its magic and then love will grow naturally and then you'll find that there's a space there and then things can flow out and change and come and go and gently things can stabilise.

It is just anxiety that wants to know in words where you are both at.

Natural trust unfolds and then you're not generating or planting seeds for future misery you're in fact planting seeds for more and more stabilisation more and more openness, more honesty, communication, ease and love.

13

Emotions Vs Feelings

W hat is the difference between emotions and feelings? Many people confuse the two, they think they are the same they think that emotions and feelings are the same and they're really not.

If you accept this distinction between your emotions and your feelings then by creating that distinction a new space, a new possibilityof being comes into play.

Emotions, everybody knows the saying 'you're never angry about what you're angry about' you're also never sad about what you're sad about. Emotions always are triggered by thoughts, something happens, your mind interprets it and the interpretation then demands you feel an emotion.

You see the puppy dog fall into a puddle and then your mind says 'oh that is so sad the puppy dog fell in the puddle' so then it tells you what is the appropriate emotion to run from your stock of unresolved emotions, through your body/mind mechanism.

However by this time you're out of the now, it wasn't a spontaneous feeling, even though the emotion sometimes feels spontaneous if you actually look it goes: recognition of what's happening, find corresponding emotion, run the emotion through your body.

The emotions are stored in your pain body and you carry them with you until they are resolved.We keep getting them triggered until they are fully felt and resolved.

When you feel sadness or grief it's always the same sadness, it's always the same grief,no matter what the circumstance that triggered it that time was.

With feelings it's different. Feelings are not there because of anything, emotions are there because of something. Your mind interprets life and because of that you have an emotion.The emotions we carry come from the past situations that happened that we didn't fully integrate the experience of at the time.

Emotions are when your mind encapsulates feelings and labels them and gives them meaning.

We generate meanings about the dramas that we've lived and we support those meanings with emotions. It's an entirely fabricated thing.

Feelings on the other hand are different, when your emotional body is cleared even if it's just for a moment,then the feeling of life,the present,the Presence emerges. It's a bit like when the movie is stopped being projected onto the screen there's just this incredible blank but that blank isn't null and void, there is a feeling, these feelings we givethem names like unconditional love, joy, gratitude, peace,clarity and freedom.

There are no negative feelings in the universe,there's no sorrow inherently existing in the universe.There's no anger inherently existing in the universe.When we become free we do not experience anger or sorrow, those are emotions and they come from misunderstanding how life is.

Angels don't get angry, angels you don't get sad, there's no fighting going on in Heaven! Why because there is no actual inherently existing cause of anger or any wholly existing cause of sorrow for one who sees what is clearly.

The fact that something dies is not sad, the fact that somebody dies is not sad otherwisewe'd all get it as sad but we don't. Some people think 'thank God he's gone" some people think 'oh my god it is so sad, he's gone' dependent on who their being that that person was to them. Their grief is given by their meanings that they have invented. The emotion of grief does not emanate from the dead person.

This is an incredible thing because we tend to look at grief or sorrow, anger, jealousy, all the different emotions that run through us, we tend to look at them as real,we give them reverence but they actually just need to be felt,they keep on returning until we do feel them. Until we do acknowledge, accept, and recognise that actually they come from somewhere way back then and are just waiting for resolution.

As we clear 'the there then' we fully arrive in 'the here now'

In the same way that with physical pain if it reaches a certain threshold we pass out, if say as a child we experience highly impactful experiences then the emotional reaction is deferred until such time as we can absorb it which we might do over years a bit at a time.

It's possible to clear the backlog of unresolved emotion to clear the pain body. It's possible toclear the backlog of unresolved anger to actually get to the core and the root of the anger,the root of the sadness and to resolve it so that you move from being an emotional person to being a person who can feel massively without a fear of being overwhelmed.

When you experience emotions it's always the one feeling the emotion and the emotion itself. When you have feelings it's only one thing that is going on,the feeling is happening,it's a living thing, it's not me feeling it,it's just the event of a clear space, a self cognising wonder, the feeling life happening.

Whereas in emotions it's me feeling the emotion, me calling the emotion up.

It's an amazing breakthrough when you get this that if you're feeling an emotion that the meaning of it comes from somewhere outside of that moment. This moment that you feel the emotion in has just triggered it for re-examination, for integration and resolution.

Causeless joy and happiness becomesstable as we clear the emotional body.

The feeling of happiness is the feeling of life and is not derived from circumstances going well but just the experience of life itself you don't really know that you're happy because you're not there measuring it and there's no commentary about it.

When you feel deep peace you don't really know the depth of that peace because there's nobody there measuring it or commentating about it .

We become increasingly stable in clarity and happiness as the emotional body empties itself and becomes resolved.

Emotions are always called forth by thought,feelings naturally arise out of presence.

Emotions are conditioned responses, feelings spontaneously appear from the heart of life.

Emotions keep returning until resolution comes, feelings of peace underscore all phenomena.

Emotions are triggered by the interpretation of events, feelings flow free from thought.

Emotions are generated in the body/mind and feelings soar in awareness.

Emotions appear in time and drama, feelings are only ever in the now.

Emotions are projected so they can be seen, feelings emerge from nothing as all there's ever been.

As we awaken, we are heading away from the turbulence of emotions into the deep world of pure feeling where the egoic self that suffers, dissolves into an ocean of feeling. The Self is seen as pure feeling, the seer, the seeing and what is seen are then one. The feeling, the feeler and what is felt are the same.

14

How To Get Over A Breakup

"The most dangerous psychological mistake is the projection of the shadow on to others. This is the root of almost all conflicts."

Carl Jung

When a relationship ends often it's easy for one partner and not easy for the other. So what is the difference? Why is it that the one who is left is the one that suffers and the one who does the leaving generally suffers less? This is because it's about choice. The one who does the leaving has chosen to act and leave and the one who is left is in reaction to his choice.

So if you find yourself in the position where someone has chosen to leave you then your best advice is to make a choice yourself. Otherwise you remain in reaction to this other person's choice. Once you make a choice yourself then you are back in action at the driving wheel of your life instead of remaining in reaction to what happened in his life. When you make a choice you reconfigure your life.

It can become obsessive,each person must be responsible, if they don't want to suffer,for really being honest and seeing when their thinking has become obsessive.It can be really hard.When thinking becomes obsessive it's no longer really about what you're thinking about it's more to do with your attachment and your craving inside yourself, what you have made the drama mean.

In the same way that grief,when someone dies, is not actually to do with the deceased but it's to do with your relationship to them, in fact the grief stops you really seeing where they're going and the beauty of their departure.

It's true that obsessive thinking about the ending of relationships and about that person stops you moving forward. It's not really about the relationship or them it's about you.

We need to see that it can become habitual so that you always start your day thinking about how it could be,what they are doing, this sets up a sense of a beingness which can be self fulfilling- that things then don't work out for me and people get stuck there.

It's important to have closure. How did you have closure in a relationship? In order to have closure, proper closure, in a relationship you don't actually need the input of the other person.Its great if you do but its not essential.The person might have died or the person might have just walked off but you can still have good closure.

The way to get good closure is to take 100% responsibility for your experience in that relationship.

No one can make you think, feel or do anything. This is the stand of power and the end of victimhood.

"Ah" you go," but he betrayed me, he went off with my best friend" well it was because of who you were being that he was that gave you how you got him.

Who you were being that he was gave you how you got him and how you got him was that he betrayed you. Not easy to accept this confronting truth.

Somewhere in there you had a blind spot that virtually invited him and gave him subtle permissions to do what he did.

So who your being that he is gives you how you get him,not everybody gets him the way you do, who you were being that the relationship was gave you how you got it. How you got the relationship was entirely different to how he got the relationship because who he was being the relationship was was different. You may never know how he got the relationship what's really important is how you got the relationship .

You can have closure when you take 100% responsibility for your experience, only then can you move on and close the chapter and begin a new one.

When the relationship initially ends then you enrol your friends in your narrative of what happened.A story which paints you as the victim and the hard done by one and leaves him at fault.We all do it but there's no closure in that.

The second stage is where you go "okay I now, in hindsight, see that who I was being that he was gave me how I got him and I had withdrawn this, I wasn't doing that, I was becoming a little bit like this,I let it be like this,I didn't respond to that etc.' and you start to see how you created this beingness which gave you the version of him that you've got now.

He also has to do that for himself and it's not about blame it's about taking responsibility,a hundred percent responsibility for your experience in the relationship.

The power comes back to you when you take that responsibility.

When you are in this obsessive mode, constantly looking backwards, constantly hoping that the past will return. At some point there has to be some discipline, at some point there has to be some wake up, you have to get bored with it .You have to recognise the consequences, by holding on you are spoiling your life, you limit your chances of happiness. Really this recognition is something that, wonderfully, can actually happen in one day.

You can be in a momentum of attachment and grieving for a long time and then one day, in one moment (maybe even now) you just get how boring it is, being that way and choose to let it go, drop it and move on.

This is the amazing thing about a choice. A good choice will reconfigure your life because a choice doesn't come from your mind.

Choice isn't born out of "should" a choice is: finally the threads of causality come together in a moment and a choice point appears and you go with it. It feels right, there is no great deliberation. The time has come, you've reached the end of that and you're ready to put it down. It is something that happens on an energetic level, on a deeper level than the mental level which is where decisions take place. It's a choice "I choose to move on, I choose to let this person go. I choose to recover my joy".

When you're constantly obsessing you're very prone then to depression. It becomes depressing because you're constantly reaffirming your root negative idea about what life is and what's not possible for you .But remember that root negative idea is only an idea that was created from some difficult causes and conditions way, way back.

It's not actually how life is. It's just who you're being that life is at the moment but once you see that you have full power back with you, no longer acting as a victim of circumstance, the circumstance of this person not being with you, you realise that actually you are the only dreamer of your life and this is the most profound realisation to have. If you can get it, if you can see this then it makes all that suffering worthwhile.

There was a day when that started, there was a period when it was at its peak and there is the possibility of a day when that stops. For me it stopped in a moment, it didn't fade out, it just stopped because I finally saw it was a psychological dynamic and once it was exposed and I owned it and I opened up to it and I admitted it, it was done.

We think "oh but I feel so much, it's got to be real" .No your feelings can be very,very deceptive.Maybe you have a feeling or an intuition but the meaning that you're giving it,that's another thing. There's the feeling and then there's the meaning you give it but the meaning is likely to be very biased by what you want.

You can't trust the meanings, you say to yourself "oh because I feel this it means she's got to be on the other end of it!" She wasn't on the other end of it she was with somebody else talking about how much she loved him, building a future with him, she was not thinking of me!

Another way the illusion manifests is that we get signs and symbols in all kinds of ways and give them meanings too. The favourite song is on the radio has some meaning, astrology, superstitions, all are given meanings to support hanging on to what we should be letting go of.We stalk them online or even in real life.We justify this nonsense and we don't really talk of it because we know its crazy but it is giving us something.We think that sometimes a little bit of fantasy love is better than no love at all.

You can do that sometimes years after they've actually gone. Years later you choose to let them go and your life reconfigures and suddenly again you're a space where new relationships can happen because the thing about holding on to past relationships and not choosing to move forward, is that you're not a place where a new relationship could really come because your heart is already taken.

You've still got the secret flame burning, you are still believing that this person will somehow miraculously come to their senses and come back. That isn't going to happen and even if it was to happen you're still better off letting go!

Waiting for what isn't going to come can create tremendous amount of suffering and it becomes a kind of mood that really clouds everything and it's surprising the number of people that feel this and I certainly have felt it, this inability to face reality. It' s like grief, there are stages of grief and to start with it's denial,the relationship has ended but you just can't believe it. I remember in particular one relationship, I thought "no way is it ended, we may not be together but it hasn't ended, she'll realise, she'll come back. I

know it hasn't ended because I' m feeling it, I'm feeling connected to her, there can be no doubt that that connection is still alive even though we're not actually together and she's actually with someone else it doesn't matter because we're still connected and it'll come round,she will be back, its destined to be!"

This of course is a delusion it doesn't come round, sometimes it might, you hear stories, but not often. But you do hear them enough to keep that delusion going "no it's going to happen, it's supposed to be, this is just a temporary glitch" but it's some years later and it's still going on.

There's a lot of denial,it feels safer to live in hope than to face the pain of the truth.

One payoff for being this way is that by living out of the past, hoping it will return,one does not have to create a future.You keep walking backwards into the future having your past inform or infect your present.

One of the ways of getting over a relationship is finding someone that you can you can have a casual sexual relationship with even if it's just once because in doing that you recalibrate your heart, you recalibrate your centres, you recalibrate your psyche. It' s a kind of magic, it doesn't always work but it can be helpful.

On the same frequency of being that you developed with the other person the psychic connection can still be there. This works for some people better than others but it's it's definitely a way.

The closure comes when you stop telling the narrative of your victimhood and take responsibility for your experience of the relationship.

Time doesn't actually heal but the healing happens within time and sometimes it takes a while to get over it but you can and then you can move on and you'll find that your next relationship will have the benefit of what you've learned by taking a hundred percent responsibility from the previous one.

If you stick with your narrative you will heal eventually but your next relationship is likely to be similar to the last containing a similar teaching.

It is a difficult time when you are broken hearted but all the people whose hearts were broken they recovered and their hearts were able to love more. So keep going, process what comes up use it as a learning experience, become strong, strong in love and the next phase of your loving relationship life will be much more successful.

In the meantime be sure to give what you want to get!

15

Individuality And Independence In Relationships

'When you say Yes to others make sure you are not saying No to yourself.' Paulo Cohelo

How do we maintain our independence and individuality in relationships? Is it true that somebody can take away your independence? Is it true that someone can take away your individuality? I don't think it is. It is true that you can have the sense of losing your independence and have the sense of losing your individuality.

When you're in a relationship you're kind of not independent, you're with somebody else and how you're being about that determines whether that's a pleasant thing or not a pleasant thing. The fact is that you're co- creating with another human being and so you have a loss of independence, you're in relationship you can't just do what you want to do, when you want to do it because you're with someone else and things get negotiated and things are shared and you give up this for that and then they give up that for this.There is consideration of the other persons needs and desires and of what it takes to keep the love alive.

The loss of independence comes with the relationship but it doesn't have to be a bad thing, it actually can be a beautiful thing that you are making those gestures of sharing and being more selfless, considering the happiness of the other.

The loss of the sense of individuality, the sense that "I'm being overwhelmed by this person, I'm not functioning as I was when I was on my own and it's because of the relationship is because of this person" that is a bit different.

Why do we lose our sense of individuality? Noone can take it from us. We give it away, we give it away because of a number of different reasons: perhaps we think that if we maintained our sense of self and our focus on our own life, then somehow they wouldn't like us. Part of the reason why people want to be with us, we might think, is because we're so amenable and will flow with what they want and so we do that but over time that builds up resentment and at some point that resentment will show itself and mostly people will blame the other person -' oh you just dominated me and so I didn't get to do what I really wanted to do with my life!'

What we have to realise is that in a dominating relationship where there's a dominator there must be one who is dominated and they are in agreement, whether consciously or unconsciously, its a synergy.

In sexual acts of domination there is a conscious agreement "okay you dominate me with the big whip or whatever and then afterwards I'll tie you to the bed and dominate you!" but that's a conscious thing.

When it happens unconsciously we make unconscious agreements with people and we communicate that by who we are being, with body language, subtle signs, we communicate that in the way that we respond to things which gives them permission to dominate us.

When we're not feeling good about ourselves we think " I have to give twice as much to this relationship in order to get half as much back because really that's all I'm worth and if I don't do that then I won't be loved" but this is again a misunderstanding coming out of a wrong identification.

If you think you are your psychological self which is full of complexes,is wounded and broken, then you will inevitably have the sense that you're not good enough. So you'll then inevitably be doing strange trade-offs in relationships. 'I'll give twice as much as you if you'll just accept me, I'll let you dominate me if you'll just love me, we'll just do what you want to do if you'll just let me do it with you'.

These kinds of payoffs, these kind of deals come out of a wounded self and the thing to understand really is that you're not wounded. That's the psychological self. That's who you thought you were. Thought has made that.

When you are feeling bad and depressed, negative thinking about yourself created negative impressions and built rooms in the house of your psychological self. Those moments where you felt really good and up, they built positive rooms in this house. But none of that actually is you and so really all this sense of identity, this sense of individuality,this sense of independence, these are all psychological symptoms and the real remedy is to know the Self.

Once you get who you truly are- the Self, you don't need anybody else to confirm who you are,because you are not offering any versions of your self, so you don't need to make any trade-offs, you don't need to make any psychological negotiations in order to get that sense of ' I am accepted' .

When you accept yourself as you are, you won't have to buy that acceptance from others, it'll just be there.It's amazing you accept yourself and everybody else accepts you and it is no longer an issue for you.

People have got too much on their own minds about themselves to be wondering about whether you're acceptable or not.If you develop self-acceptance you will be accepted.

So losing the sense of individuality it's not losing it, you haven't lost it you've given it up which is a bit more confronting and you've given it up for a reason because you think that that's what you need to do in order to be loved, validated and accepted. Then you will attract people, who will fulfil that need in you, so if you've got a need to give up yourself, you'll find someone who'll want to take it. You just magnetise them to you, they'll turn up and that drama will play out so then your relationships are created subconsciously. It's an unconscious attractive force that brings these people to you but once you see that and you let go and move forward then you can start attracting conscious relationships with people who actually match you and the future you are choosing to live into. They are not an aspect of your psychodrama, you are not projecting onto them, you're actually just present with them as beings so it grows, flows and love wins.

Codependence is where two people have collapsed into each other and they both have given up their individuality to please the other, to create the relationship because they mistakenly think that that's what it takes. What happens there in a codependent relationship is it just gets gradually more and more boring until there's no freshness, there's no growth and there's just simmering unexpressed resentment. Codependent relationships are psychologically based and do not really allow for love

All these things you can move on from once you see them, once you make them conscious then you can move forward. In relationships remember love brings up anything unlike itself for the purpose of healing so if you find yourself in one of these dynamics it is not signifying that the relationship you're in isn't viable and workable, it's signifying that something has come up for healing and with communication and with introspection and with honesty and love you can move forward and clear it.

16

How To Deal With Rejection

"I don't want anyone who doesn't want me."

— Oprah Winfrey

W e have it that rejection is bad and it really does not have to be. Our body does not hurt when we get rejected, it's not our heart that gets hurt when we're rejected it's just our ego. The ego is definitely reprogrammable.

Imagine what fun you could have if you chose to have it that rejection was fine with you! Youcould approach people who you thought were way above your play grade!

If someone rejects you it's not your problem it's their problem,they're missing out on you, they're missing out on the chance to know you. You who are unique, you are as good as anybody else, you are wonderful because you're alive and you love in a unique way. If they don't want you that's their choice, they're allowed to choose. You can't make them choose you, they're allowed to choose or not choose you but it doesn't mean anything about you that they don't choose you.

It means something about them. This is the important point, it doesn't mean that you are not good enough because somebody doesn't choose you. They could not choose you because you remind them of their mother or a past lover or perhaps they feel the dynamic between you is too strong and that they might loose control and become overly vulnerable.

They could not be choosing you for all kinds of subtle reasons that they may not even be present to, none of which actually relate to how you get yourself.

You have to also trust it, so that when you get rejected by somebody maybe there's a distinction here between what you fancy and what would actually work for you and this person saying no is actually serving you.

At some point when you kind of recover from the rejection you have to take the view 'I am hundred percent responsible for my experience in this life, so somewhere within me I generated that rejection, somewhere in me that response from life matched who I'm being that I am in some department of myself and that's needs to be looked at.'

Actually you get there's nothing about your body or your personality even that would itself create rejection. You see people who are more ugly who didn't get rejected or people whose personalities are less attractive who also didn't get rejected. So it's much more about who your being that you are that gives you how you get yourself and your life.

You set yourself up for that and what it does is that it proves right a negative idea you have about yourself. So you remove that negative idea once you see why you've got it there and then you'll find that rejection doesn't happen. You are no longer a place where rejection happens.

There's no fixed thing about a person that gets them rejected, it's not like a fixed fate. Infact there isn't anything fixed about us which is really good news!

As there's nothing fixed about you, if you get rejected once, twice or whatever it may have seemed like "oh I'm never good enough, nobody's ever gonna choose me" or whatever, you are generating that.

If you don't take that view,you can choose not to take that view, then the other option is that you're a victim of other people which leaves you powerless and sitting in a place of ' I'm not good enough' and it proves that right.

Then you think that you are not good enough more and so then it turns up again proving it even further right. But actually it's not true it's just who you are being that you are in that moment and historically.

One thing you can do is love, it's good to know that about yourself. Whatever happened in your past or however your personality has turned out at the moment, youcan love and you can love in the way that only you can love and that actually is something pretty amazing and mustn't be forgotten. You are lovable, you have to go right back to the basics and get that you're lovable, that you're loving, you're a lover and that you love love and that isn't damaged.

The personality, the psychological self has all kinds of wounds in it and dysfunctions and complexes but where love comes from isn't damaged, you can love and even if you get it that you're damaged or broken or battered by trauma and all that has happened, still there are people out there who will love you exactly as you are right now.

You don't have to present a perfect self in order to be loved. In fact don't even try to present a perfect self, just recognise that you're lovable not for any particular reason, you're just loveable that's just how it is.

Someone could love you and then you don't have to kind of act because a lot of times people get rejected because they turn up one way on the first day and they've got their act on and by the third date things are beginning to wobble and the fourth date doesn't come because the person goes " I don't really feel that person, something not right there"

because they're acting. When we are who we are and present

vulnerabilities, who we are then makes it much easier for love and acceptance to happen.

So how to deal with rejection? Don't take it seriously, don't take it personally and then after a little while recognise that somehow who you're being that you are is generating that rejection and you're doing it for a pay off.

Perhaps one part of you says 'I just really want to be in a relationship' but another part which might be hidden, actually doesn't. So it creates a situation and a set of behaviours that will definitely get you'd rejected. So that you don't have to face what the fear might be of intimacy or the fear of being known or the fear of having your selfishness exposed or the fear of just connecting with another human being or the fear of being hurt and abandoned again.

Love is amazing! Love is truly amazing it's the one thing that no one can really speak about because it can't be grasped or looked at but what we do know about love is that it it'll come out of nowhere whenever it wants to and people who have spent years thinking that they're never going to be loved get loved and it can spark in the most extraordinary way, at the most extraordinary time.

One thing that encourages love is kindness, so if people give what they want to get it encourages love to arrive but you can't really do anything to bring love forth. There's tremendous hope because you don't have to be a certain way, you don't have to change.

You could be loved exactly as you are, people just want to be accepted .

Accept ourselves as we are, accept the fact that sometimes we are like this, accept the fact that sometimes were like that, accept other people, accept that they're like this, accept that they are like that, all that anybody wants really is just to be accepted as they are- a work in progress.

As soon as you accept things as they actually are, a situation, a person you'll find connectedness. But if you're meeting someone and you're judging them mentally and anxious about whether they're judging you or not and not really accepting them as they are then they pick up on that and it can cause intimacy not to happen.

17

Why Don't Some Relationships Work?

"Who you are being that relationships are gives you how you get them."

Werner Erhardt

Why do people find themselves in unhealthy relationship dynamics?

There are two ways you could look at this basically one answer to that question is that it's just bad luck,the universe just dealt their cards that way, that explanation leaves one disempowered and without any understanding, its fatalistic.

Another view is that who you're being that something is gives you how you get it. Who you're being that something is gives you how you get it. Who you're being that relationships are gives you how you're getting them. When we say 'who you're being that something is' what we mean by that is who you're being that something is is what you're thinking about it both consciously and unconsciously, the space you are for it, are you a place where it could happen?

What is that space that you are for it ? A jungle of brambles or is it a clear open space where something could happen, an inviting space? Do you have room in yourself for another? Is the possibility of meeting someone activated or have you closed it down?

'Who you're being that something is' is every single way that you are about that person, situation or possibility, your body language, your thoughts, your eye movements, your breathing patterns, your relationship to past memories concerning that matter, what you're saying about it, what you're thinking about it, what you're doing about it. All constitutes 'who you're being that it is'.

Some times people think that this statement is incorrect grammatically and that it should be "How.." not "Who". That is who they are being that it is so they get it as nonsensical and wrong! The statement contains profound truths, it's "who you are being" because to say "How" would infer that there was a fixed someone who was being a certain way. This is not the case when we look within we do not find anyone just Awareness. Who you are being is the identity you are now, the only time where you actually exist.

Now who you're being that you are determines how you turn up for yourself, so for example. If you have it that you are who you think you are (the psychological self), then you're inevitably going to be feeling that somehow you're not quite good enough and probably to counter that, the idea that your somehow 'special' and better than others in some way. Because that's who you're being that you are you'll probably also be being that way that your life is, and consequently what will turn up is something that proves that right. Which will be a dysfunctional relationship, proving your primal thought, that you're not good enough, as correct. If we see it that way we can examine who you are being that relationships are and get really present to all aspects, having done that then it's possible to transform it such that we consciously choose to be a different way that relationships are and have them turn up for us differently. Because there is no fixed way that relationships are for you regardless of how it appears.First you have to see who you are being, then see why and then you will be able to transform.

Also on our journey there are aspects and meanings that we've created in the past, for example if our primal programming about relationships was from our parents who had a very dysfunctional one, then the programming that we have about relationships from a deep level may not be a good one. So we may find ourselves living that out until we can consciously see 'my god I'm just living out the programming I got from observing my parents, from the meanings that I created'.

Who we are being that something is, also means the meanings that we've given it, for example, we are a child or young, and our first love affair goes badly wrong. It ends traumatically, we inappropriately give too much or our heart is broken or we get betrayed. The meaning we can give that, and this is common, is that you might say 'somehow I don't quite have the relationship software that others have and that's why they never work for me and they never will, that's just who I am' .

So we create a meaning that is like a self- fulfilling prophecy, we attract people that exactly match who we're being that relationships are for us but it really is coming out of only a meaning that we created and perhaps a misunderstanding and a misinterpretation in a time of trauma way back then.Its not the truth about you and relationships.

People notice that they have similar relationships that keep on occurring and that again makes them think 'oh I always get the wronguns and I always end up getting cheated on,or I always end up getting attacked violently.'

One person who came to see me had a succession of five relationships with what looked like really nice people. Each one of them ended up beating her up. She got to see that she was the common factor.She saw she was subtly presenting herself as a clearing for those kinds of people. She saw it was relevant that her parents had a violent aspect to their relationship which she was witness to.It never occurred to her that the experience of seeing her parents behave that way had created who she was being that relationships were and was the cause behind her attracting those violent relationships.Once it became conscious she was able to transform her experience of relationships.

The relationship you're in directly corresponds to something in you. Never mind the other person, you're never going to know what that other person is about, you will never know them as they know themselves.

Like you, there is no fixed way that they are, it's not really your concern, look to yourself if you're in a dysfunctional relationship. If you're in a violent relationship, if you're in a relationship that's not working look to yourself, that's where the answer is and once you find who you're being that relationships are such that they turn up that way, then you can transform them.

This is what's amazing because there isn't a fixed way that you are in the matter of relationships or in the matter of yourself or your life. There's nothing fixed so once you see how you've crystallised and solidified it then you can transform who you are being such that relationships turn up differently. I've seen that, I've lived that, seeing beings having tremendous breakthroughs in who they're being that relationships are such that they turn up in a new functional way.

Dysfunctional relationships have an enormous amount to tell us on our pathway of growth.

However where there's violence, physical violence, then you have to really think what is this? Why am I attracting this to myself? Is this really what I want? And make some good choices because if you transform who you're being that love is, that relationship is, it will turn up for you differently.

Please understand that when I say 'who you are being that relationships are gives you how you get them' and you get them as violent and abusive I am not saying it's your fault or blaming you. I am attempting to show you the way out of that beingness and thinking that attracts these things to you unconsciously.

Sometimes it is the right thing to be courageous and just leave and get help. People think 'I'm so ugly or I'm crazy that I cant really hope to attract somebody so I have to take anybody who who will have me because I can't be alone' but the thing is this, you know that if you live like that, if you think like that then that is what will happen but it's still not the truth about you.

Actually because you're a human being you're really good at loving that's something you can do, you can love that makes you worthy of someone who can receive it.

You can love and you can have a loving relationship whatever your mind is saying, whatever meaning you've told yourself from the past about you in relationships just put it down.

18

How To Stop Thinking So Much.

"If you get the relationship to the Self right,all other relations will work"

Elijah El- Shaddai

I s it possible to control the mind? Is it possible to control our thoughts? The truth of the matter is that pretty much all of our suffering comes from the mind. There's no other portal that suffering comes into our experience except through the mind, except through our thoughts.

Even if we have intense physical pain it can be viewed just as a sensation its what we make it mean that brings us suffering.

There are some people who have very intense physical pain but they make nothing of it they just experience it and then there are others who have very little physical pain but make a lot of it and suffer.

It is how we think about life and how we think about ourselves that causes us suffering.

Is it possible to control our thoughts and where do our thoughts come from? The first thing to understand perhaps is whether or not we are the thinker.

Are we the thinker or are we the one that is witnessing the thoughts? Where do the thoughts come from? Do we always think from the same place?

Are our thoughts more trustworthy sometimes than at other times? If they are more trustworthy sometimes than others what determines that?

A lot of people are thinking 'oh I'm always thinking, it's always me thinking'. In other words all my thoughts come from the same place and it's me thinking them.

Where do the thoughts come from has been the question of deep meditators, people who sit still for a long time looking at and observing and inquiring into a question like that. What they have reported and what I can confirm from my own experience, is that the thoughts arise spontaneously of their own accord,given by who I am being that life is in any one moment. If I'm being that life is a cause of anger my thoughts will spontaneously arise as angry for as long as I'm in the beingness of anger. If who I'm being is unconscious, I'm not present, I'm just unconscious then my thoughts will be a reflection of that, they will arise spontaneously as unconscious thinking.

There are two ways I can go with my thinking either I' m awake in which case I'm choosing my thoughts or I'm unconscious and what is not resolved by me what is still cooking in theunconscious of the experiences that I've had, that takes over my thinking.

Carl Jung, the great psychologist, said that what you're unconscious of drives your life.What you're unconscious of drives your thinking unless you take ownership of your mind. If you take ownership of your mind it means to be awake.

The mind has two basic functions,one is to think and create thought and the other is to focus.

Perhaps this a key to the answer of the question ' how do I control my mind?'.

There is a story that comes from India that I really like:

One day there was a guy and he was traveling along a path and he stumbled upon a cave and he thought that it looked interesting so he went into the cave and lay down and dozed off. When he woke up he noticed something shining and he uncovered it and it was a genie's lamp.

As he held it he saw something engraved, it said 'rub me'.So he gave it a good rub and the next thing he knows with a great cloud of smoke this genie has appeared!

The genie says 'oh master thank you for liberating me I've been in this lamp for a long time.I'm here to give you anything that you want'.

Well the guy, he can't believe his luck, he's thinking 'okay let's get out of here I want to get to the the city, I want to get there right now.'

The next thing he's transported there. The genie comes and says 'hey master what would you like now?" He said "I need somewhere to live, build me a great palace" and suddenly there's a great palace built.

He's just about to sit down and the genie comes and goes "hey uh what can I do for you now?" and then the guy goes "okay let's have a big dinner and great people and dancing girls and you know everybody looking fantastic and get some music going!"

So the genie has manifested it all he's just about to sit down and eat something and the genie is tapping his shoulder again "master what's up?" and he replies "hey let me enjoy this" and the genie goes "no you've got to keep using me that's how it is, you've got to keep me going."

So after about two weeks he's hadn't had any sleep he's got about 10 palaces, he has everything he can think of. He is at his wit's end because he's not actually able to enjoy anything that the genie has given him.

He tells his friend, he's got a real problem. The friend says "well you know there's a there's a holy man,there's a sage sitting not far from here, why don't you go and see him?"So he gets the genie and he goes and sees him.

"Oh great one please help me, I've got this genie who gives me everything that I could possibly want I just have to speak my desire and it's instantly manifest but I have no peace.I have no chance to enjoy anything because it's always demanding from me something to do, what shall I do? How can I resolve this problem its driving me mad?" The wise man gives a thought for a moment and then he replies: " build a tall tower and when you're not using the genie you tell him to go up the tower, get to the top, turn around and come back down again and then go back up to the top and turn around and come back down again until such time as you need him." Well the guy thinks that's just great and he does that and so he gets to enjoy all the things that the genie has brought for him and when he doesn't need the genie the genie is given that task.

This points to something very important because when we're not using our mind it will use us.

If you tell your mind to shut up will it? No because you're not in control of it, if you tell it to stop it won't stop will it? It carries on, you're not in control of it because you're not the thinker you're the observer of those thoughts.

We need somewhere to put the mind when we're not using it consciously otherwise unconscious material is expressed in our thoughts and we find it overlaps onto our living experience. Unresolved material gets projected onto people; say we haven't resolved something with our mother then it gets projected onto a woman we might meet.Or say we haven't resolved some issue of anger then it gets triggered by all kinds of things that happen in the life.

So when we're not focused into the now, into presence, into who we truly are then our mind processes unresolved unconscious material and our thoughts become filled with that and the thoughts can get so powerful that we lose consciousness of what this moment actually contains.

There are different techniques, some people just stay with their breath and the tower is the breath going up, up, turn around and come down,down so you put your mind and focus into being with your breathing.

More subtly and more wonderfully you can focus on and feel Awakeness.

19

What Is Awakeness?

"Are you dreaming you are awake or awake dreaming your life."

Anon

Awakeness is the limitless feeling of life in this now. Being freedom, being clarity. Attending to awakeness you give your attention not to your thoughts but to being awake to the feeling of life itself and that awakeness, then multiplies.

The more we attend to awakeness the stronger it becomes.

The more awake we become the easier it is to identify when our mind is trying to hijack us.

In meditation many people say 'oh I can't meditate because I just drift off, my mind it never stops' but you don't actually know whenthat's happening do you? You sit down and you've got an intention to focus in a particular direction but somehow two or three minutes or half an hour later you realise that you've drifted off and your mind captured you and took your attention away from where you chosen to put it and took it off in a completely different direction.

The more you concentrate on awakeness, the fact that you're alive, the presence of suchness, the feeling of being, the easier it becomes to identify your mind. The next stage is that you develop some absorption.

To start with if one focuses on a flower most people won't be able to focus on the flower or the candle for very long before their mind drifts off.

But you can develop your capacity to focus and concentrate and as you do the next stage emerges. You choose to rest your attention on something and you put your attention on it and it stays there. You just rest your attention in a relaxed way and it just stays where you put it. On the periphery you may hear your mind producing thoughts but your attention is resting in a relaxed way.not wandering off but still where you put it and then an amazing thing happens, the heart opens and you come out of the place of chatter and your attention goes into the heart. A profound silence develops as your attention returns to its source and in that silence there is no thinking.You are absorbed in the heart, awake and conscious.

What this shows us is that it can't be right that we are entertaining all this thinking, all the time. Drink a cup of coffee, somebody upset you and you're thinking and thinking and thinking and thinking and thinking and thinking and nothing comes of it. It is not like anything good has come of it. It can't be right to have this beautiful body, to be in this paradise planet and yet not to be able to experience it because we're completely captured by thinking and internal dialogue.

Thinking that we are the thinker.

There must be a remedy to this and there must be a purpose for that endless thinking. The purpose is to get us to come to the conclusion that this isn't right and there must be something more. There must be a place that I can live from that isn't filled with chatter and there is.

Once we get that then how we can do that, the way that's right for us, will appear.

It can be very, very simple, as simple as putting everything else down,for a moment and recognizing the natural state.

What is the natural state? Is there any thinking happening there?Is there a lot of unconscious chatter there?

No, that is the beautiful awakeness to what life actually is. There is this distinction between the mind and the heart, they're not really two but it can help to see them as such.

You're not the thinker, the thoughts are generated and arise spontaneously of their own accord given by who you're being in any one moment. You are the witness of that and interestingly the more you become the witness the harder it is for unconscious thoughts to invade your reality. Then your capacity to only think as you choose increases and a momentum of peace, a momentum of silence is always nearby, it's closer and closer until you can just want it and it's there, it's instantly there.

That peace and that silence is just the most wonderful thing,it is the divine and the mind is silenced and focused, the mind is focused there completely focused and absorbed.

There are physical pain hells but there's also mental hells that people experience. What to do if that is happening for you? Find somewhere to put your attention. The simplest solution is to put your attention consciously somewhere else consciously listen to music, perhaps put your attention into nature,it works every time for me. No matter what I'm feeling if I go into nature I start to feel something wonderful, this beautiful world.

If it's an intense storm then perhaps put your attention into repeating a mantra and this brings the mind back in your control. Mantras can focus the mind when the mind is all over the place being hijacked by obsessions, hijacked by rabid thinking and emotions.

Constant psychological self-assessment is not the path to self-knowledge it is the path to hell.

It's important that you realise the wonder of the fact that you're not the thinker.

This is a major stage on the path to Freedom.

When you realise this you cease to be quite so bothered about what you think,there is something better going on for you.

You begin to see that if you're feeling upset your thoughts will be upset, if you're feeling moody, you're going to have moody thoughts, if you're feeling traumatised, you're going to have traumatised thoughts and you're going to invent a meaning with those thoughts about life and about yourself.

Then afterwards you're going to remember the meanings you invented in the time of trauma and you're going to think that they were insights and that they were reality. But they weren't, they were born of trauma and this is why a lot of people suffer beyond the moment of their trauma because they make up meanings for themselves and about life in the moment of trauma which stay with them.

Follow your thoughts back to your heart, the cave of your heart and there is a profound silence, the origin of the sense 'I am'.

The lake is completely still in that place and in the centre of the lake is a shining diamond.

20

What Is Freedom?

"Do not interrogate silence because silence is mute; do not expect anything from the gods, not should you try to bribe them with gifts, because it is in ourselves that we must look for liberation."

Buddha

Why don't I always feel free? The one that asks that question is never going to be free, it doesn't know what freedom is. It experiences relative states of consciousness arising out of different circumstances and gives a commentary. 'Oh I feel so free today look I'm surfing the waves! I'm so free!' It'll give you relative degrees of how free you feel,' ah I don't have to work today I feel so free'. You are taking your reference from this internal dialogue from this commentary and that is why we suffer. That is why our experience of life is so limited.

Freedom is different from that. The fact of the matter is freedom is always there and you are that. Every time you look for freedom it's there, every time you put what isn't freedom down, it's there. Why am I not always feeling free because you're dreaming and in the dream freedom is something quite different to what it is in reality.

There are two modes that we can live by either we are a cartoon character going birth to death like a waveform and our identity is supported by internal commentary and judgment or we're in Presence awake in this now .Every single time we come into Presence our heart opens and we arrive in the moment there is blossoming freedom and we realise that it's not 'I experienced freedom'. I am that freedom. If I put everything that I'm not down I realise that truly what I am is that freedom.It is the basic ground of being.

What we mean by freedom: something that is unobstructed, something that has no limits,like the sky. Something that is not bothered by anything else, something that is supreme pleasure.

So the one that asks the question it's filled with complaint, it thrives on complaint and basically at some point we've got to get to the place where we feel so done with spending time listening to that internal dialogue.There comes a point where the dawn finally comes and you recognise that thinking is only relevant when you are consciously using that capacity. That you have consciousness to think with. When you're unconscious, a dream character, flowing along, it just produces thoughts spontaneously out of who you are being. You don't even realise it and you're sitting there not even realising that you're sacrificing being freedom for listening to that nonsense which is just your mind talking to itself.

In this realm there really is no joy, no love and no peace.

All it does is limit you and take the colour out and bring everything into a set of relative values, everything's got a value.

The happiness in that realm is for a reason determined by the internal dialogue.

Freedom is not coming, freedom is there when you're authentically and truly and really want it and choose it. To the point where you'llactually put down what's caused you the problem, even for a moment,and there is freedom that spaciousness that unfolds that fizzing, wonderful peace that comes. That Presence that you dissolve into that is freedom and it thrills the heart.

21

The Self And Mental Health

"All that is required to realise the Self is to Be Still."

Ramana Maharshi

What is the Self? Who is the one that knows you're thinking these thoughts?

The one that witnesses the confusion is that one confused or moved at all?

The witness is the deepest part of you, it remains unassociated with all it observes,unchanging as the sky.

How do you shut up the internal dialogue? Can you tell it to shut up by creating anothercharacter and talking to it? No, you can't tell yourself to shut up it won' t happen.

How do you know it's not you thinking because it won't shut up when you tell it that's how you know it's not you ?

If it was you and you told yourself to shut up then you would shut up. When it is rabbiting on,what's the only way that you can shut it up?

The only way I found is to distinguish myself as the listener. You can't have your centre of focus in two places at the same time. Either your central focus is in the chattering or it's inthe listening. As soon as it comes into the listening chattering stops for as long as it's in the listening.

Start with getting a sense of the observer who has never been tainted by anything that's happened. Then your relationship with all the characterisations and characters that get stirred up by spontaneously arising movements of your mind becomes easier to deal with.

You see the truth of it is that if we really get down to brass tacks, right down to the very, very deepest, that which you've always been,which we must call you, can't have bad mental health or even good health.

It's the domain in which all that happens, just like the sky is the domain within which weather happens. Bad weather one minute, sunny the next minute. All of it happens in the sky but never changes it.

What does that equate to in us? That sky like awareness the domain in which all your feelings thoughts and actions take place.

When you go into a cinema and a movie is projected on the screen, we all completely forget it's a movie, it's just like projected onto a screen they're not really gonna kill the hero, the world doesn't really end, it's a movie but we release our emotions and we project our past and our emotions, our ideas, our aesthetics and every kind of thing onto the screen. People crying the whole cinema is screaming at the same moment .I've seen it and then at the end the screen is still there unchanged nothing happened to the screen no matter what was projected on it. Is there something like that in me? If I knew of that would that transform my relationship to my mental health?I think it would.

Its good to remember everything actually does change.No weather condition remains, sometimes the conditions last a long time it is true but nothing is immune to change, nothing remains the same, no mental state, no mental ill health or dis-ease remains without changing.

It passes, it changes, it moves but that which observes remains the same and unassociated.

Sometimes just remembering the certain truth it is going to change can be helpful for me. From my experience, which is all I can really speak from authoritatively, is that if you want to help your own mental health the best possible thing you can do on a daily basis is to sit still and get good at being at peace, get good at putting down stuff, even for a few moments is good.

"What you practice, whatever it is, you get good at."

Prem Rawat

So even if when you first try to meditate all you hear is the chatter of your own mind that's just the beginning. Then you practice and then after a while you start to understand from a very deep place how it works and what's really going on and how simple it is to be at peace.

The whole universe is filled with deep peace if you went out a thousand miles into deep space and got out you would feel everything in deep stillness.Deep, profound unfathomable stillness that's where we need to rest and keep returning there and then after a while we start to realise that "I am NOT my mental health! That's not who I am!"

Who are you? "oh I'm a schizophrenic! Who are you? I'm a bipolar? Who are you I'm a whatever". No, you're not that's your mental health condition. Who you are that's something to find out and funnily enough, amazingly enough, luckily enough who we truly are has not really got that much to do with our mental health.

So returning to this place starting to recognise peace within realising that the mind will always be chattering but I don't have to always be listening. I can take my attention and put it into this place of the listener, the witness.

I can recognise something wonderful within me. When you're having very bad mental health that peace actually is still there because you are present in this body, at any point in this life and you can return to Presence once you've got it. Once you've seen it you can return to Presence very easily and then it feels like I am being supported by an unknown force. Who is that? What is that that just brought me out of something and unfolded something else for me? There's a lot more love around then we recognise and remember.

I think for good mental health it's really important to communicate because when your mind tells you stuff and you believe it that's when things go strange but if you told that strange stuff to somebody else, when you say that in another person's listening, it's a very subtle thing but you kind of get their reality on what you're saying and it allows you to not to be quite so involved in what you're saying.

Communicating, allowing people to listen to you so that you can hear yourself.

The key thing is the understanding that no matter how bad the weather internally the sky of awareness does not change. Peace is with you always.

22

Self Validation

"Be who you are and say what you feel, because those who mind don't matter and those who matter don't mind."

Anon

How do we validate ourselves? How do we self validate or how do we get over the need to do it?

When you truly are who you are the Self there's absolutely no need to validate it. If you're standing in glorious sunshine you don't have to get someone you who is passing by to confirm thats what is happening, no it's absolutely blatantly obvious that you are standing in sunshine.

When you have to validate or get people to agree with or get people to support you that isn't who you are. It's the latest version, it's got all its qualities that you're puffing up that you're pushing forward saying to the world this is who I am,and hiding the stuff you hide which becomes the shadow. So a deal goes on 'I'll accept your projection of yourself as you if you'll accept mine'. But this isn't who we are and it's never satisfied. It takes a lot of work to get validation, as soon as people sense that you need it,they tend to withhold it or use to manipulate you.

If you want validation from lovers it's not happening and even if you get it it doesn't feel right because it is still isn't who you are. When you get it you realise that validation from others does not quench the existential thirst.

So again the real question is who are you? What is the Self?

The first thing we have to get on that journey to Self Knowledge is that the constructions we've made to answer that question psychologically: 'oh I'm the one that was wounded in the past' or 'I'm the one that's got this special talent' or' I'm the one that nobodylikes' or' I'm the one that everybody loves' whatever, that's not who you are.

The part that you play in the movie of your life it's not who you are. You might be a mother, a woman, you might be spiritual, you might be a great lover. None of these things is who you actually are, that's the part that you play.

The Self is something else. Behind the ego is the Observer, that's the first stage. The first stage is to recognise that you're not the ego,you're not who you think you are.

That identity that is built of thought, it isn't you that's your attempt at making yourself something but it's not who you are. You are behind that, you are before that and you will be after that.

The first stage after the ego is to get that you're the Observer, you're the one that listens to your thoughts and is unmoved by them. You're the one that is behind your eyes looking out dispassionately. You're the one that your senses report to.

To find that one and rest as that one and become that one is the goal. When you do that then the part of you, the ego-self, the invention, your projection into this world, the part that you've been playing, it starts to dissolve.

You don't need it anymore, it was a big trouble because when you are identifying as the part you play it's very hollow, there's not joy there,

there's not peace there and only a very conditional kind of love.

So validation is only needed when you're being who you're not! Because really you know it's not true so you need someone else to tell you that it is so you feel better.

Moving on from that is Awakening.

The awakening is realising that you are the Observer. The Observer is not moved by anything that you think, the Observer doesn't care at all about anything it's completely impartial, it just sees everything. It just feels everything,observes and witnesses everything. The states of consciousness are witnessed by the Observer, your thoughts are witnessed by the Observer, your feelings are witnessed by the Observer which is prior to the ego and is complete and whole.

To become self validated means to feel the Self, the true Self behind the ego, when you relax into that sense 'I am' then all the validation you need is right there in that moment, you feel complete and real.

We seek to get validated because we feel somehow incomplete so we think 'oh if I just got everybody else to agree with who I say I am then I would be who I say I am'.

You are something else, the Self and that's the journey. The journey of Awakening is moving from the ego self into the true Self, the witness, the observer.

23

Families And How To Survive Them!

"Until you have completed your relationships with your parents,all your relationships will be about your parents".

Werner Erhard

Why do we get triggered and how can we complete our relationships with our family members? What does that even mean?

'Completing your relationship' means getting over yourself, bringing it all into present time, recognizing what you've been projecting on them all this time, stop living out of the past. 'Completing' means seeing them as they are and the key is accepting them as they are but it's very hard sometimes.

Why do we get triggered? Let's look at that first. We get triggered because often it is our family who has witnessed us creating our identity and most people in our lives that we meet believe our identity that we project out but our family have a history, have a different version, an opinion, a judgment and they're the hardest ones to convince that we are who we're now projecting ourselves to be.

Our family are the ones who in our formative years were most likely around us and had a part in the traumatic things that happened. In our trauma we invent meanings about them that tend to stick.

When I was very young, when I was six years old, my mother sent me to boarding school and I didn't know why. She sent me to boarding school because that's what they did in those days and she thought it was the best thing for me. But as a young boy I thought it must be because I was bad.

I thought maybe she doesn't love me because I'm bad, maybe I'm being punished for something.I didn't know what, so I created all these reasons. I started to believe that she didn't love me, that she didn't want me at a very formative age, and I lived in that conversation with myself about not being good enough, about being bad and being unloved and unwanted. I lived in that conversation which was born out of trauma and not true but I lived in it for decades. It infected my relationship with my mother and in the latter days before the healing came I couldn't spend any time with her without having a blazing argument there was tremendous friction between us.

Then I did this process where I looked at my complaints of my mother 'she's so selfish, she hasn't got time for me, all she's got time for is herself, she does not love me'. Then I was directed to look at the payoffs for me holding those complaints. How did it benefit me psychologically holding these views of her because I had it that it was her fault that I wasn't who I thought I should be. I had it that it was her fault that my relationships were going the way they were going and I had it it was her fault that basically my life was not as it should be. The payoff in seeing her as the cause of my failures was that I got to be right, to not have to be great, not have to make an effort, I could play victim and not take responsibility for my choices and have it all be her fault.I could judge her, I could punish her, I could withdraw my love and project and transfer my stuff onto her.

When I realised all this it was quite a revelation, I saw that I was just making it all her fault and playing the victim of course I was completely powerless to do anything, a victim can't do anything except complain.

Then the question was what has it cost you being this way about your mother? What does it cost you and I realised it cost me everything. It didn't feel good in myself because I wasn't being authentic I was caught up in a kind of projection, transferring my unresolvedness onto her and punishing her by withdrawing my love. So it didn't make me feel good, made me not self-expressed, it made me kind of stuck as a six-year-old child even though I was an adult. (This is something very interesting to look at where you are stuck, what age are you stuck waiting for resolution?)

So then what did it cost me? My relationship with myself, it also cost me my relationship with my mother, the one from whom I came into this world, who gave me the greatest gift of all. It also infected everything else because if you don't deal with your primal relationships, with your mother and your father, then you play them out everywhere, Play them out with the police, with other men, you play them out with authority figures, you act them out with women and with people who look like your mother, anybody can trigger those issues until they're resolved. That's what was happening to me.

People think 'okay what I'll do is I'll just ignore my parents and I'll never speak to them again" so they leave and think that's a way of dealing with the dysfunction but it isn't. I was meeting my mum in other women. In fact I started to meet my mum with pretty much every woman and the issues that I'd had with my father,I had a very bad relationship with him for a while, was projected onto all kinds of authority figures.So you can't get away from what has to be accepted, what has to be understood, what has to be released.

People sometimes say 'oh I did have a big problem with my dad but he's dead'. He maybe dead in the physical way but he's still a character in your psyche that you need to come up to speed with, complete with.

The completion is when you come to the place of closure, and this is the same within relationships as well, it's not just with your parents or your family members this is in all relationships.

When is a relationship or a chapter closed? How do you get closure? People say 'oh I haven't got closure". How do you get closure? You get closure when you can take 100% responsibility for your experience of that person or of that relationship.

How I got my mother was given by who I was being that she was.She did not get herself that way and nor did anyone else.

Other people didn't argue with her every time they met her. Some people really liked her.

She was very popular, people would call her up and speak with her but I got her that way. Towards the end of that phase it was literally horrific. I couldn't be with her more than three or four minutes before this deep rooted anger that I wasn't really in touch with would be triggered by something really small,like the way she was sitting would trigger me or the way she wouldn't share the tv remote! It would trigger me and all the boiling, unresolved anger towards her coming out of who I was being that she was which was that she was bad and wrong for putting me in boarding school, would bubble up.

The healing came when I realised that who I was being that she was gave me how I got her. She wasn't actually that way, and people go 'no, no, she actually is that way, both me and my sister, we agree she is that way!'. No she's not because the real truth is there isn't a way that she is, everyone gets her differently, she got herself differently each time she encountered herself. Who I was being that she was gave me how I got her and who I was being that she was was contaminated by what had happened in the past and what I made of it and the meanings that I'd invented. I invented those meanings that I wasn't good enough that she didn't want me, that she didn't love me, that she was bad and she was wrong. I invented all those meanings it wasn't the truth about her, it wasn't how she necessarily saw herself or how other people got her. I got her that way. Who I was being that she was that was the cause of my misery. I had transferred my stuff onto her.

This is what I began to see that I had projected my stuff onto her and why? For the payoffs.

To access the payoffs I asked myself ' who do you get to be by being this way about your mother' and ' by being this way who don' t you have to be?'

'What don' t you have to do because of being this way? What am I trying to prove by being this way about my mother? Who am I attacking by being this way? How do I get to be right by being this way?'

Who did I get to be by being this way about my mum? I got to be right, spiritually superior, I got to be rebellious, I got to play victim, to be selfish,I got to withdraw, I got to sulk,I got to not have to be great, I got to be lazy and not have to commit to a future.There were all kinds of payoffs that came with this way of being but obviously the cost is always much greater than the payoffs.

Exposing this then I started to see 'oh my god it's who I'm being that she is that gives me how I get her and that's why I'm so angry but really she is not the cause of anything.

She gave me birth it's quite the opposite, it's because of her that I've got everything.

I began to see that if I played the victim 'oh I was sent away to board in school at six and it's affected me forever' and 'I'm damaged and my my inner child is broken'. If I stayed there I would be like that because that was who I was being that I was.

It wasn't the truth about me, the inner child is not actually who you are, it's a construct in the psychological self to explain certain behaviours, it's not a real thing. So if I maintain that position then I would be stuck as a victim.

When you're a victim it's only when you take responsibility that you can you can start shifting stuff so then I did. I realised I am responsible for how I feel, it was me that projected onto her, it's not my business who she is to herself, I'll never know how she gets herself.I will never know how my father gets himself. I can only ever be looking at them from the outside in but they're living from the inside out. It's the same the other way around my mother will never know how I got myself, she could intuit things but she could not know. In that sense we're alone because only I am in here looking out.

How to Let Love Win!

24

The Completion Conversation

"To err is human, to forgive divine"

Alexander Pope

Who I'm being that my mother is has given me how I got her.I can transform who I am being that she is having recognised whatwas actually going on.

So I did and I called her up because that completion, that realisation happened in a day and I called her up and said 'mum I need you to listen to me just till I've finished and then I'll listen to you without interruption.I don't want to argue with you I just want to say something'. She agreed to listen.

I said 'look mum I've realised something amazing, I've realised that I blamed you for everything and coming out of what I made it mean that you sent me to boarding school when I was so young. I blamed you and had that be the cause of everything that's wrong in my life,it's your fault and it's not fixable and that allowed me to space my life right out. I blamed you but I've realised it wasn't your fault at all. The truth is you did what you thought was best for me and even if you weren't keen on parenting for whatever reason that was just who you were at the time doing the best you could and I have come to this place where I accept you as you are, you're a work in progress and I'm a work in progress and I accept you as you are and where forgiveness is needed I hope that you can forgive me and I forgive you. I realise that my unresolved self has got in the way of me seeing you as you actually are and so who I was being that you were, part of that beingness, meant that my perspective of you was warped, it wasn't a clear seeing and that's why it's been so difficult but I want you to know that I've got over that now and that I see you and I forgive you and I accept you as you are". I said to her 'you know it's cost me a lot and it's cost us a lot holding on to this and the new possibility that I want for us, for the rest of our time together, that we can be happy and loving and care for each other'.

Now my mum was a great talker she talked all the time never caught short for a comment to make! When I had finished that there was this silence on the phone. Then I went "mum are you there' and after a while she said 'I can't imagine in my whole life hearing anything more wonderful than that".

Two three weeks later, I went to see her and I was a bit nervous about it. As it turned out it was just beautiful being with her, it was all fresh and new and simple. Then we had about 20 years more that she remained alive and we never argued in that way again. There was no more friction between us we had accepted each other and out of that acceptance came a beautiful life and so when the time of her passing came, I was there and leading up to it there was a lot of love between us, nothing really needed to be said it was just a feeling of completion and after completion there's just love.

After the work's been done then you've got time with that person then how beautiful, you can just be in a beautiful place with them. This is what it looks like when Love wins..

91

So how do we complete the relationship? We take full responsibility for whatever we felt and the meanings we created and we unconditionally accept and forgive the other and ourselves for being who they were.

Accepting someone as they are is not making them wrong for being who they are right now and were then.

It is no small thing when you come to accept them, when you stop resisting them because you think they are not as they should be. The confronting truth about acceptance is what you can't accept about another is your stuff.

You can be carrying a judgment that costs, you in terms of how you interact with somebody, for years and decades. Then you come to the place where in one moment this completion can happen, you accept them as they are, it's not your business to judge them and punish them by withholding your love. You accept them as they are right there and then a freedom can come, a release can come. Those moments are heaven sent don' t miss them!

To to err, to make mistakes, is human but forgiveness is divine. It's the same with acceptance, it verges on the miraculous, when we accept ourselves 'okay I'm not who I thought I should be or could be or whatever but I accept myself as I am, I accept the darkness in me, I accept the light in me, I accept the brilliance in me, I accept the stupidity in me. I accept all that I am. I am like others a work in progress'.

When that moment for acceptance comes recognise it and do it because you can let go of a huge amount of baggage just like that.

I believe in what I call Rapid Breakthrough Therapy! When you're ready you can choose to put your burden down, when you're ready you can complete and restore love with your parents and your family or somebody who you've had issues with for a long time. Once you accept them and take responsibility and realise that who you're being that they are is giving you how you're getting them. And you're choosing to be that way about it because it serves you in some subtle perhaps hidden way. Look to yourself, you're not going to change them. Your position of judgment and withdrawal of your love, for their own good, hasn't changed them at all.

A lot of what underlies our resentments andfrictions in our families is we think we're better than the other, we think we're more clear than the other, we think we're more spiritual which we think gives us license to judge and so we do, we find them guilty.

Having found them guilty we have to punish them and the most popular way to punish those we love is to withdraw our love. A lot of the time we withdraw really because we don't want to look in that mirror because it's too bright. Lovers and families can be very confronting sometimes!

One thing you should never forget is that your mother loves you above and beyond everything that may have happened.

Don't forget that your father loves you above and beyond everything,and that is the truth the heart knows,and it will never change and whatever has happened doesn't change that.

We all make mistakes, we all have regrets of things that we've said and done. So completion comes when you can accept people as they are.

When you can accept yourself as you are. We're not static or fixed,look at yourself, you're not static are you? You're always changing, you're evolving, you're understanding, you're growing and if you get earnest about that you'll experience it more whatever you age.

You can transform your relationships when you realise that how you get them is given by who you're being that they are. What kind of space you are for them,what you're allowing them to be? I was a place where where my mother couldn't be her shining self I wouldn't allow it, in the way that

I was being.

This understanding of 'who you're being that something is gives you how you get it' is crucial, it's a revelation that gives you power and victimhood is then over.

The price of completion is forgiveness of your self and all others, knowing that if you had experienced their exact causes and conditions you would have done the same thing.

25

When Is A Good Time To Restore The Love?

"Never put off until tomorrow what you can do today!"
Shri Hans Ji Maharaj

I f you ask your heart am I ready to forgive? Am I ready to accept? What's your heart going to say? Is it ever going to say ' well not quite no' ?

No, as soon as you ask your heart 'am I ready?' Its going to say 'go for it!'

Trust Love, you're such a beautiful being, come with love, full acceptance and full forgiveness.

Restore the love.

If you're not having good relationships it's probably because you haven't restored the love with your parents.

Restore the love with your parents and you'll no longer have to act out that unresolvedness in your relationships with others and then your relationships get freed up and you stop bleeding your unresolved psychological self into them and you can just love in present time.

What if the other party isn't ready? You have no way of knowing that and you thinking that can be a subtle way of manipulating the situation so that you don't have to move from your heart.

It doesn't require them to be ready for you to accept them, for you to forgive them, for you to open up and own who you've been that they were that gave you how you got them.

Even if they're not ready, you trust the universe, somebody can become ready in a second. Your loving intention can make them ready and even if they're not it doesn't really matter because your expression will help them either way.

It's a fantastic thing when you restore the love. When you Let Love Win!

Tremendous love is there, I realised 'I do love my mother, she does love me and this psychological nonsense has been in the way.' It was such a relief for us both.

Sometimes we actually have to say to somebody 'I accept you and I'm sorry", sometimes we actually have to forgive people consciously not just rely on awareness and time to sort it out. We actually have to take some responsibility, we have to say what is in our hearts and recognise that our perspective is contaminated by who we are being that we were.

Often it's hard because our ego is involved, we make it into a thing about winning and losing and right and wrong. Whereas really who we want to be is the one who restores love, the one who gives the victory to love, that's winning!

'I am going to do this'! How beautiful that's you choosing to let love win. That's your resolve, that's who you are. Your choices define you, define the part you play in this life. Will there be help from hidden places in the doing of that? Will angels walk with you when you move to restore love? I think so.

I'm not speaking from theory here this has happened to me and I want to share this possibility with you so that you can complete your relationships and you can restore the love.

For about 20 odd years after the healing I had with both my parents, we were complete, fully complete and there was love and no resentment and everything was expressed and we were in present time, loving. Before that it was horrendous and dysfunctional.

You know you can, there's never been a better time.

Literally no blame, no judgments. Who cares? Your judgments are heavily biased, they say everything about you and not much about them.Its about putting down your story because you get that its really just that.

Loving, forgiving, accepting, sharing that's the beautiful you, no ill comes from that. Everything else is questionable but no ill comes from being the loving being that you are.

How do you make sure you don't slip back into old ego driven ways and patterns that are so long established?

Don't worry about it just try and be awake. When I restored the love with my mum it wasn't 'I resolve to be nice', it wasn't about resolutions, they don't work do they? You say 'I'm going to give up smoking on New Year's day' and then by the evening you've got a cigarette on!

It's not a resolution to be nice and to forgive. You have to be authentic about this you have to really see what's being said and how it actually is. Then there can be transformation. Transformation is like a caterpillar turning into a butterfly. There's no going back from transformation, it's not a mental thing, it's deeper than that, it's an authentic seeing that you're having about who you've been that that person was and you're recognizing, for real, that it was who you were being that they were that gave you how you got them.

Then it's for real but if it does slip back, you never give up, you keep going, you keep going in the name of Love.

Contact:timaeontalks@gmail.com

Printed in Great Britain
by Amazon

82825029R00056